100 Poems
to See You Through

100 Poems
to See You Through

Bright Words For the Darkest Hours

EDITED BY
DAISY GOODWIN

EBURY
PRESS

1 3 5 7 9 10 8 6 4 2

Published in 2014 by Ebury Press, an imprint of Ebury Publishing

A Random House Group Company

Text compilation © Daisy Goodwin 2014

Daisy Goodwin has asserted her right to be identified as the editor of this
Work in accordance with the Copyright, Designs and Patents Act 1988

The Random House Group Limited Reg. No. 954009

Addresses for companies within the Random House Group can
be found at: www.randomhouse.co.uk

A CIP catalogue record for this book is available from the British Library

The Random House Group Limited supports the Forest Stewardship
Council® (FSC®), the leading international forest-certification organisation.
Our books carrying the FSC label are printed on FSC®-certified paper.
FSC is the only forest-certification scheme supported by the leading
environmental organisations, including Greenpeace.
Our paper procurement policy can be found at:
www.randomhouse.co.uk/environment

To buy books by your favourite authors and register for offers visit:
www.randomhouse.co.uk

Project editors: Helena Caldon and Nicola Crossley

Original design: Peter Ward

Printed and bound in the UK by CPI Group (UK) Ltd, Croydon, CR0 4YY
Typeset by SX Composing DTP Ltd, Rayleigh Essex

ISBN 9780091958176

Contents

FOREWORD

MAGGIE'S CENTRES provide free practical, emotional and social support for people with cancer and their families and friends, offering a programme of support that has been shown to strengthen physical and emotional wellbeing during the course of treatment. Built in the grounds of NHS hospitals, our centres are designed by leading architects to be warm, welcoming and full of light and open space. They are places to find practical advice about benefits cancer patients and their carers are entitled to; places where qualified experts provide emotional support; places to meet other people or to simply sit quietly with a cup of tea.

Great design and architecture is vital to the care that Maggie's Centres offer and so we work with world-renowned architects like Zaha Hadid, Richard Rogers and Norman Foster, who give their time for little or nothing. Their skills deliver the calm, uplifting environments so important to the people who visit and work in our centres.

The first Maggie's Centre opened in Edinburgh in 1996. There are now 19 centres across the UK, as well as help online and abroad, with more developments planned for the future.

Every year 300,000 people in the UK are diagnosed with cancer, facing tough questions, exhausting treatment and difficult emotions that can range from anxiety to loneliness and isolation. These challenges affect not only the person with cancer, but their family and friends, too.

At Maggie's, creative writing is a key element to the support we offer and poetry often becomes a way to explore the thoughts, ideas and emotions that a cancer diagnosis can bring.

100 Poems to See You Through means so much to us at Maggie's, and we hope it can bring solace, laughter and companionship to everyone who needs it.

Laura Lee
CEO, Maggie's Centres

INTRODUCTION

M Y FIRST VISIT to a Maggie's Centre was in the spring of 2013. It was a sunny day and as I cycled into the grounds of Charing Cross Hospital I looked up at the rows of windows and thought how much harder it must be to be stuck in hospital when the weather is fine. But that feeling fell away when I walked into a warm terracotta-coloured building tucked into a corner of the hospital's car park that faced the Fulham Palace Road. Designed by Richard Rogers, one of the many great architects who have designed these centres, this building is an oasis of light and serenity in the most unlikely setting. With its natural materials and thoughtful use of space, it is a million miles away from the utilitarian concrete of the hospital proper. It even smelt different: of camomile and honey rather than antiseptic and floor polish. Behind one door I could hear a yoga lesson in progress, in another corner a group of people were drinking tea around a wooden table.

My mother had died the month before and I had spent the earlier part of that year wrestling on her behalf with the many indignities of cancer treatment. Her illness – pancreatic cancer – was swift and ferocious: diagnosis to death was a matter of weeks. There was no time for her to benefit from the soothing atmosphere of a Maggie's Centre, but I know she felt strongly about the importance of beauty in extremis because, together with her partner Richard MacCormac, she had designed a Maggie's Centre in Cheltenham.

The centres offer emotional support to cancer sufferers: from psychotherapy to the comfort of simply sitting around a table with others in the same position. The graceful spaces and soothing colours make them places of sanctuary. I think poems can offer the same kind of solace. In Coleridge's phrase, 'the right words in the right order' can give a shape to the most complicated feelings. Cancer sufferers and the people that love them are caught up in a tornado of unmanageable emotions; my aim with this collection is to show them poems that might in some small way illuminate, guide, fortify and soothe them through this most difficult journey.

There are poems here to chime with every stage of

illness and recovery, hope and despair, life and death. Poets who have had cancer and other dread diseases have written with astonishing candour about all the wrinkles of their sojourn in the vale of ill health: whether it is hair loss or MRI scans, voluble nurses or patronising doctors, small-hour terrors or tiny miracles, there is a poem here that will provide a handhold in this strange new world. Jo Shapcott, Julia Darling, Raymond Carver have spun their misfortune into talismans for their readers. I would not presume to say that any poem can provide comfort but I think they can bring solace. Nothing is more terrifying than the unknown; the poems in this book, I think, provide a map of this unfamiliar territory.

Some of the poems in this book should be read silently, but there are some that demand to be read aloud. One client of a Maggie's Centre said that he found reciting from Tennyson's 'The Charge of the Light Brigade',

> Half a league, half a league,
> Half a league onward,
> All in the valley of Death
> Rode the six hundred

to be his magic bullet in the face of medical unpleasantness.

One of the things that people living with cancer and other serious conditions stress is the wisdom that comes from dealing with a life-threatening illness. For that reason I have included two sections – 'Small Pleasures' and 'How to Carry On' – which deal with the insights that come from being ill and the change in values the experience can bring about. Jo Shapcott's poem 'Procedure' is a hymn to the hard-won joys of living in the present. I particularly love Elizabeth Bishop's poem 'The Fish', which touches obliquely on the carapace we gain from experience.

Many of the poems here are for people facing illness, but I have also included poems for those who watch and wait by their side. When my mother lay dying it was difficult to know how to behave. A hundred years ago deathbeds would not have been unfamiliar to most people, but today we are as squeamish about our mortality as the Victorians were about their sexuality. There are some helpful poems here by Julia Darling about the correct demeanour for a hospital visit, as well as others that may offer some help in the midst of grief. I have lost count of the times that I have had emails from the bereaved desperate for the right poem to read at a funeral or memorial service; so I have tried to include a selection here that can be used in times of need.

But while there are, inevitably, lots of poems here that deal with the really tough stuff, I also want to include light with the shade. I think the impulse to find a seam of humour even in the grimmest situation is part of the human condition. However bleak the outlook there is always something to laugh about. The Hilaire Belloc poem about the unfortunate demise of Henry King from chewing little bits of string – '[The doctors] answered, as they took their Fees, there is no Cure for this Disease' – has been my mantra through many interminable stints in waiting rooms.

No one faces illness or tragedy in the same way. Some readers may feel they need the spine-stiffening resolve of a poem like 'Invictus', others will find more relief in the quiet acceptance of 'Wild Geese' by Mary Oliver. What is universal is the feeling of recognition that the right poem at the right time can bring. Poems work on many levels; there is the ostensible meaning and then there is that ineffable combination of sound and rhythm that works at another level entirely. It doesn't matter if you don't understand every nuance of a poem; the most important thing is to experience it. Reading aloud may feel awkward but there is no better way to get under the skin of a poem. Sometimes phrases will lodge in your memory, baffling you at the time,

XIII

but later their meaning unfurls like one of those Chinese tea balls that turns into a fully-fledged flower when you add water. Allow these poems to permeate your consciousness and the rewards will come.

The aim of the Maggie's Centres and this anthology is the same: there is always a place for beauty in the most difficult time. Whether you find inspiration, courage or acceptance here, I hope that the poems in this book will make your particular hard time easier to bear. These truly are poems to see you through.

 XIV

ACKNOWLEDGEMENTS

I would like to thank all my friends on Facebook, Twitter and elsewhere who suggested poems for this anthology and to Peter Kravitz and the users of the Maggie's Centres who helped guide me in the right direction. A special thank you to Sally George who read this book in hospital and gave it such an enthusiastic response. I am indebted to Gail Rebuck for starting the ball rolling and to Carey Smith and Nicola Crossley for making it happen. As ever my wondrous agent Caroline Michel made everything easy as did my incomparable assistant Rachel Street. But the biggest thank you must go to all the poets who have allowed me to reproduce their work for nothing, especially Carol Ann Duffy and Wendy Cope who found some new poems down the back of their respective sofas.

THE BAD NEWS

ONE MINUTE the worst thing that can happen is that you can't find a parking space and then, out of the blue, a doctor will take you aside into a private room or the phone will ring in the middle of the night and everything changes – suddenly the ordinary world of parking spaces seems like a vanished dream.

I particularly like the poem in this section by the great American short-story writer Raymond Carver, where he ends up thanking the doctor that gives him the bad news, 'habit being so strong'.

THE HEALTH SCARE

WENDY COPE

I'm living with Uncertainty and Fear.
I need to say their names and make them rhyme.
Two monsters. I can't make them disappear.
I'm living with Uncertainty and Fear.
Though abstract nouns are not a good idea,
And abstract nouns with capitals, a crime,
I'm living with Uncertainty and Fear.
It helps to say their names and make them rhyme.

END GAME

BRIAN COX

The day they said 'your cancer's worse'
I walked away through rows of limes
whose autumn leaves recalled old verse
I'd learnt by heart in better times.

Lawrence came first: his Ship of Death;
the falling fruit like drops of dew
scatters across the hardened earth.
And then there's Keats: a rosy hue
on stubble plains, moss'd cottage trees.

As I recalled these well-known lines
music of verse reshaped my news:
a touch of joy in grievous times.

GETHSEMANE DAY

DOROTHY MOLLOY

They've taken my liver down to the lab,
left the rest of me here on the bed;
the blood I am sweating rubs off on the sheet,
but I'm still holding on to my head.

What cocktail is Daddy preparing for me?
What ferments in pathology's sink?
Tonight they will tell me, will proffer the cup,
and, like it or not, I must drink.

OF MUTABILITY

JO SHAPCOTT

Too many of the best cells in my body
are itching, feeling jagged, turning raw
in this spring chill. It's two thousand and four
and I don't know a soul who doesn't feel small
among the numbers. Razor small.
Look down these days to see your feet
mistrust the pavement and your blood tests
turn the doctor's expression grave.

Look up to catch eclipses, gold leaf, comets,
angels, chandeliers, out of the corner of your eye,
join them if you like, learn astrophysics, or
learn folksong, human sacrifice, mortality,
flying, fishing, sex without touching much.
Don't trouble, though, to head anywhere but the sky.

Devonshire Street, W.1.

John Betjeman

The heavy mahogany door with its wrought-iron screen
Shuts. And the sound is rich, sympathetic, discreet.
The sun still shines on this eighteenth-century scene
With Edwardian faience adornment – Devonshire Street.

No hope. And the X-ray photographs under his arm
Confirm the message. His wife stands timidly by.
The opposite brick-built house looks lofty and calm
Its chimneys steady against the mackerel sky.

No hope. And the iron knob of this palisade
So cold to the touch, is luckier now than he
'Oh merciless, hurrying Londoners! Why was I made
For the long and painful deathbed coming to me?'

She puts her fingers in his, as, loving and silly
At long-past Kensington dances she used to do
'It's cheaper to take the tube to Piccadilly
And then we can catch a nineteen or twenty-two'.

WHAT THE DOCTOR SAID

RAYMOND CARVER

He said it doesn't look good
he said it looks bad in fact real bad
he said I counted thirty-two of them on one lung before
I quit counting them
I said I'm glad I wouldn't want to know
about any more being there than that
he said are you a religious man do you kneel down
in forest groves and let yourself ask for help
when you come to a waterfall
mist blowing against your face and arms
do you stop and ask for understanding at those moments
I said not yet but I intend to start today
he said I'm real sorry he said
I wish I had some other kind of news to give you
I said Amen and he said something else
I didn't catch and not knowing what else to do
and not wanting him to have to repeat it

and me to have to fully digest it
I just looked at him
for a minute and he looked back and it was then
I jumped up and shook hands with this man who'd just
  given me
something no one else on earth had ever given me
I may even have thanked him habit being so strong

ULTRA SOUND

PENELOPE SHUTTLE

But I only looked at the screen
when the doctor asked the nurse –
freeze that, will you?

And saw a smoky sea roaring
silently inside my breast,
a kneading ocean of echo-scape,

resonant-surge of sombre waves,

like the Falmouth sea
at autumn twilight, smudge
of grey surfs and bruise-black billows,

grainy shadow-sea inside me,
soundless thump
of seismic wave after wave

9

breaking over two black rocks,
harmless cysts,

and below, mute, storm-bleak,
the long black trembling scarp of suspect tissue.

THE WHITE COATS

DOCTORS NO longer have the god-like status they once enjoyed. Thanks to Google, everyone can become an expert on their own condition. It is tempting either to blame doctors for not doing enough or to believe that they can do the impossible, but, sadly, doctors are only human. I like W.H. Auden's definition of a good doctor as 'partridge-plump'. I think we all deserve 'an endomorph with gentle hands' to make the medicine go down.

Doctor Fell

TOM BROWN

I do not love thee, Doctor Fell.
The reason why, I cannot tell;
But this I know, and know full well,
I do not love thee, Doctor Fell.

 12

GIVE ME A DOCTOR

W.H. AUDEN

Give me a doctor partridge-plump,
Short in the leg and broad in the rump,
An endomorph with gentle hands
Who'll never make absurd demands
That I abandon all my vices
Nor pull a long face in a crisis,
But with a twinkle in his eye
Will tell me that I have to die.

THE MICROBE

HILAIRE BELLOC

The microbe is so very small
You cannot make him out at all,
But many sanguine people hope
To see him through a microscope.
His jointed tongue that lies beneath
A hundred curious rows of teeth;
His seven tufted tails with lots
Of lovely pink and purple spots,
On each of which a pattern stands,
Composed of forty separate bands;
His eyebrows of a tender green;
All these have never yet been seen –
But Scientists, who ought to know,
Assure us that they must be so …
Oh! let us never, never doubt
What nobody is sure about!

WAITING ROOM

U.A. FANTHORPE

I am the room for all seasons,
The waiting room. Here the impatient
Fidget, gossip, yawn and fret and sneeze. I am the room

For summer (sunburn, hay-fever, ear wax,
Children falling out of plum trees, needing patching);

For autumn (arthritis and chest coughs,
When the old feel time worrying at their bones);

For winter (flu, and festival hangovers,
Flourish of signatures on skiers' plaster of Paris);

For spring (O the spots of adolescence,
Unwary pregnancies, depression, various kinds of itch):

I am the room that understands waiting,

With my box of elderly toys, my dog-eared *Woman's Own*s,
Permanent as repeat prescriptions, unanswerable as
  ageing,
Heartening as the people who walk out smiling, weary

As doctors and nurses working on and on

Henry King Who Chewed Bits of String, and Was Early Cut Off in Dreadful Agonies

HILAIRE BELLOC

The Chief Defect of Henry King
Was chewing little bits of String.
At last he swallowed some which tied
Itself in ugly Knots inside.
Physicians of the Utmost Fame
Were called at once; but when they came
They answered, as they took their Fees,
'There is no Cure for this Disease.
Henry will very soon be dead.'
His Parents stood about his Bed
Lamenting his Untimely Death,
When Henry, with his Latest Breath,
Cried – 'Oh, my Friends, be warned by me,
That Breakfast, Dinner, Lunch, and Tea
Are all the Human Frame requires ...'
With that, the Wretched Child expires.

OUT-PATIENTS

(FROM *CHANGING THE SUBJECT*)

CAROLE SATYAMURTI

Women stripped to the waist,
wrapped in blue,
we are a uniform edition
waiting to be read.

These plain covers suit us:
we're inexplicit,
it's not our style to advertise
our fearful narratives.

My turn. He reads my breasts
like braille, finding the lump
I knew was there. This is
the episode I could see coming –

although he's reassuring,
doesn't think it's sinister
but just to be quite clear ...
He's taking over,

he'll be the writer now,
the plot-master,
and I must wait
to read my next instalment.

INSTITUTIONAL BLUES

I T IS easy in hospital to become obsessed with the details – the angle of a chimney pot seen from a hospital bed, the particular squeak of a nurse's shoe, the tardiness of the newspaper trolley; better to think about the small things than to hover over the abyss. The more a hospital is like a *Carry On* film, as in Pat Borthwick's poem 'The Ward Mouth', the better. Distraction is all.

NURSES

JULIA DARLING

Slope-shouldered, bellies before them
the nurses are coming, garrulously,
they are bossing me in and out of clothes
into windowless rooms, tucking me in.
Nurses are patting me, frowning,
then they guffaw in another room.
They have flat-footed footsteps
and very short memories.

But I am the woman who won't take off her bra,
the one who demands that you look her in her eyes.
Miss Shirty, they call me, I know my own veins;
when they come back for me, I'll be gone.

How to Suss Out the Night Staff

CATHERINE GRAHAM

Ward 1
Do not ask anyone
who only smiles with their face:
They are on auto-pilot.

When you need iced water in the night,
ask the one who sings
Beach Boys songs to herself in the kitchen.

Join in:
Bar Bar Bar Bar Barbara Ann …

Harmonise:
Bar Bar Bar Bar Barbara Ann …

Then, for you are now best friends:
'Any chance of a top-up?'

Rockin' and a reelin' Barbara Ann
Bar Bar Bar Barbara Ann …

FIVE O'CLOCK SHADOW

JOHN BETJEMAN

This is the time of day when we in the Men's ward
Think 'One more surge of the pain and I give up the fight',
When he who struggles for breath can struggle less strongly:
This is the time of day which is worse than night.

A haze of thunder hangs on the hospital rose-beds,
A doctors' foursome out on the links is played,
Safe in her sitting-room Sister is putting her feet up:
This is the time of day when we feel betrayed.

Below the windows, loads of loving relations
Rev in the car-park, changing gear at the bend,
Making for home and a nice big tea and the telly:
'Well, we've done what we can. It can't be long till the end.'

This is the time of day when the weight of bedclothes
Is harder to bear than a sharp incision of steel.
The endless anonymous croak of a cheap transistor
Intensifies the lonely terror I feel.

NOTHING

SELIMA HILL

Because she is exhausted
and confused,

and doesn't want to argue,
and can't speak,

she dreams of nothing
for a thousand years,

or what the nurses cheerfully call
a week.

LOCAL

GREY GOWRIE

Shrub scrub
between Radiography
and where nurses live;

our small sub-
wood: stage flat with two or three
beech, one silvery

birch, holly and laurel and then
the fox mangy lawn
beyond Outpatients – we thrive

on natural scraps:
slivers, like these;
like the halogen

mist of a moon
over Pharmacy;
the drowsy syrups

Tramadol, *Zopiclone*
which blind night ache,
or the borrowed sun

in our north-faced room
fooling the mind's eye and heart's care
that summer when

the E Ward woodpecker
did strut and take
light on his breast and burst into green fire.

Malade

D.H. LAWRENCE

The sick grapes on the chair by the bed lie prone;
  at the window
The tassel of the blind swings constantly, tapping the pane
As the air moves in.

The room is the hollow rind of a fruit, a gourd
Scooped out and bare, where a spider,
Folded in its legs as in a bed,
Lies on the dust, watching where there is nothing to see
  but dusky walls.

And if the day outside were mine! What is the day
But a grey cave, with great grey spider-cloths hanging
Low from the roof, and the wet dust falling softly from them
Over the wet dark rocks, the houses, and over
The spiders with white faces, that scuttle on the floor of
  the cave!

Ah, but I am ill, and it is still raining, coldly raining!

AFTER VISITING HOURS

U.A. FANTHORPE

Like gulls they are still calling –
'I'll come again Tuesday. Our Dad
Sends his love.' They diminish, are gone.
Their world has received them,

As our world confirms us. Their debris
Is tidied into vases, lockers, minds.
We become pulses; mouthpieces
Of thermometers and bowels.

The trolley's rattle dispatches
The last lover. Now we can relax
Into illness, and reliably abstracted
Nurses will straighten our sheets,

Reorganize our symptoms. Outside,
Darkness descends like an eyelid.

It rains on our nearest and dearest
In car-parks, at bus-stops.

Now the bed-bound rehearse
Their repertoire of movements,
The dressing-gowned shuffle, clutching
Their glass bodies.

Now siren voices whisper
From headphones, and vagrant
Doctors appear, wreathed in stethoscopes
Like South Sea dancers.

All's well, all's quiet as the great
Ark noses her way into the night,
Caulked, battened, blessed for her trip,
And behind, the gulls crying.

WARD MOUTH

PAT BORTHWICK

The Ward Mouth knows everybody's business.
The Ward Mouth knows all the nurses' names
and all the nurses' boyfriends' names.
The Ward Mouth knows to the minute
when everything should happen –
Breakfast, Coffee, Lunch, Tea Break, Dinner, Night Drink.
It said so on the form.
The Ward Mouth knows *all the little tricks* –
like *how the windows open* and *how to change the angle of the bed.*
The Ward Mouth knows what all the shifts are called
and that they are all *eight hours long*
except for *Nights* which are *two hours forty minutes longer.*
The Ward Mouth has been on
or knows somebody else who has been on
or knows somebody else who knows somebody else
who has been on every medication in the Drug Book.
She tells the Junior Houseman what he ought to do

and then tells everyone else
she *had to tell the Junior Houseman what to do*.
She can't understand what the Overseas Doctors say.
She announces this to everyone
except the Overseas Doctors.

The Ward Mouth is in the bed next to mine.
She keeps tugging my curtain back,
says it stops her seeing *one end corner of the ward*.
The Ward Mouth can't understand my need for privacy.
She thinks I'm aloof, calls me *Lady Jane* almost behind my
  back.
The Ward Mouth has been in here many times before.
There is not much left of her except her mouth
and, just occasionally, her fearful silence.

Unspeakable

THE POINT of poetry, especially at the worst of times, is to give a shape to our most incoherent thoughts and feelings. Medical professionals will ask you to rate your pain on a scale of one to ten, but poets can do better than that. Hugo Williams' description of his pain, as a dog 'grinding its teeth in my flesh' is horribly precise. Is pain senseless or does it confer wisdom on the sufferer? I like the image of the scarred fish in Elizabeth Bishop's eponymous poem that endures 'until everything was rainbow, rainbow, rainbow'. Finally, there is the battle cry against pain that is 'Invictus', which W.E. Henley wrote in 1875 following the amputation of his foot (he was suffering from tuberculosis of the bones). Although this was Henley's second amputation, he recovered and went on to have a successful career as a writer, as well as being an inspiration to Nelson Mandela during his stint on Robben Island.

THE DOG

HUGO WILLIAMS

A dog has got hold of my arm
and is dragging me down.
Its canines pierce an artery.
Its entrails twitch with my blood.

Whenever I am brought in
for further questioning,
the dog stands over me,
grinding its teeth in my flesh.

It's like being nailed to the floor
and told to relax.
Blood spurts like a confession.

This is what dogs are for,
to find out who you are.

I watch its eyes going round,
analysing the evidence.
I'll admit to anything.

AFTER GREAT PAIN, A FORMAL FEELING COMES

EMILY DICKINSON

After great pain, a formal feeling comes –
The Nerves sit ceremonious, like Tombs –
The stiff Heart questions 'was it He, that bore,'
And 'Yesterday, or Centuries before?'

The Feet, mechanical, go round –
Of Ground, or Air, or Ought –
A Wooden way
Regardless grown.
A Quartz contentment, like a stone –

This is the Hour of Lead –
Remembered, if outlived.
As Freezing persons, recollect the Snow –
First – Chill – then Stupor – then the letting go –

INVICTUS

W.E. HENLEY

Out of the night that covers me,
Black as the pit from pole to pole,
I thank whatever gods may be
For my unconquerable soul.

In the fell clutch of circumstance
I have not winced nor cried aloud:
Under the bludgeonings of chance
My head is bloody, but unbowed.

Beyond this place of wrath and tears
Looms but the Horror of the shade,
And yet the menace of the years
Finds and shall find me unafraid.

It matters not how strait the gate,
How charged with punishment the scroll,
I am the master of my fate:
I am the captain of my soul.

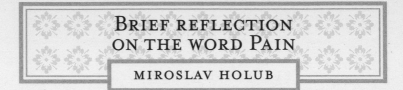

Brief reflection on the word Pain

MIROSLAV HOLUB

Wittgenstein says: the words 'It hurts' have replaced
tears and cries of pain. The word 'Pain'
does not describe the expression of pain but replaces it.
Thus it creates a new behaviour pattern
in the case of pain.

The word enters between us and the pain
like a pretence of silence.
It is a silencing. It is a needle
unpicking the stitch
between blood and clay.

The word is the first small step
to freedom
from oneself.

In case others
are present.

PAIN

ELIZABETH JENNINGS

At my wits' end
And all resources gone, I lie here,
All of my body tense to the touch of fear,
And my mind,

Muffled now as if the nerves
Refused any longer to let thoughts form,
Is no longer a safe retreat, a tidy home,
No longer serves

My body's demands or shields
With fine words, as it once would daily,
My storehouse of dread. Now, slowly,
My heart, hand, whole body yield

To fear. Bed, ward, window begin
To lose their solidity. Faces no longer
Look kind or needed; yet I still fight the stronger
Terror – oblivion – the needle thrusts in.

THE FISH

ELIZABETH BISHOP

I caught a tremendous fish
and held him beside the boat
half out of water, with my hook
fast in a corner of his mouth.
He didn't fight.
He hadn't fought at all.
He hung a grunting weight,
battered and venerable
and homely. Here and there
his brown skin hung in strips
like ancient wallpaper,
and its pattern of darker brown
was like wallpaper:
shapes like full-blown roses
stained and lost through age.
He was speckled with barnacles,
fine rosettes of lime,

and infested
with tiny white sea-lice,
and underneath two or three
rags of green weed hung down.
While his gills were breathing in
the terrible oxygen
– the frightening gills,
fresh and crisp with blood,
that can cut so badly –
I thought of the coarse white flesh
packed in like feathers,
the big bones and the little bones,
the dramatic reds and blacks
of his shiny entrails,
and the pink swim-bladder
like a big peony.
I looked into his eyes
which were far larger than mine
but shallower, and yellowed,
the irises backed and packed
with tarnished tinfoil
seen through the lenses
of old scratched isinglass.

They shifted a little, but not
to return my stare.
– It was more like the tipping
of an object toward the light.
I admired his sullen face,
the mechanism of his jaw,
and then I saw
that from his lower lip
– if you could call it a lip
grim, wet, and weaponlike,
hung five old pieces of fish-line,
or four and a wire leader
with the swivel still attached,
with all their five big hooks
grown firmly in his mouth.
A green line, frayed at the end
where he broke it, two heavier lines,
and a fine black thread
still crimped from the strain and snap
when it broke and he got away.
Like medals with their ribbons
frayed and wavering,
a five-haired beard of wisdom

trailing from his aching jaw.
I stared and stared
and victory filled up
the little rented boat,
from the pool of bilge
where oil had spread a rainbow
around the rusted engine
to the bailer rusted orange,
the sun-cracked thwarts,
the oarlocks on their strings,
the gunnels – until everything
was rainbow, rainbow, rainbow!
And I let the fish go.

SIDE-EFFECTS

NOBODY WANTS to be ill, and then to be blasted by gamma rays and have all your hair fall out; but at least poets can view the awful nitty-gritty of illness as material. Novelists can use their imagination, but poets have to write from the heart. I was so impressed by the courage and humour shown by poets like Julia Darling, Dorothy Molloy and Jo Shapcott, to name but a few, in the work they have produced while being seriously ill. I love the humanity of Jo Shapcott's ode to baldness, 'Hairless', and the wry last line of 'Radiotherapy' by Dorothy Molloy.

RADIOTHERAPY

DOROTHY MOLLOY

Nurses feed the nuclear machine that hovers
overhead with lumps of lead.

Vast areas of me are thus protected from the beams,
or so it seems. Between each session

Kathleen and Olivia, Aileen, May and Margaret
take turns to push my pelvis round

about, ensuring that the rays will hit their target.
The side-effects are as expected,

but for one: my pubic hairs fall out.

PROSTATE

BRIAN COX

My doctor's young, but still his words
reflect old-fashioned courtesies.
He shyly says: 'You'll lose desires',

averse to break the social code
which covers up a hidden world:
erections in the marriage bed.

And so at night we lie here chaste,
a little sad for what is lost,
yet all the memories we share

create a stillness richer far
than happy bouts of push and thrust.

HAIRLESS

JO SHAPCOTT

Can the bald lie? The nature of the skin says not:
it's newborn-pale, erection-tender stuff,
every thought visible – pure knowledge,
mind in action – shining through the skull.
I saw a woman, hairless absolute, cleaning.
She mopped the green floor, dusted bookshelves,
all cloth and concentration, Queen of the moon.
You can tell, with the bald, that the air
speaks to them differently, touches their heads
with exquisite expression. As she danced
her laundry dance with the motes, everything
she ever knew skittered under her scalp.
It was clear just from the texture of her head,
she was about to raise her arms to the sky;
I covered my ears as she prepared to sing, to roar.

Haiku

CLAIRE KNIGHT

chemo over
the pink water lily you gave me
begins to open

spring sunshine
catching your fine regrowth –
watering maiden hair ferns

ANOTHER BOX OF NIPPLES ARRIVED TODAY

CHAR MARCH

The hospital computer's gone mad
– that's the third box this week.
You stick them on the fridge door,
the phone, the handle of the kettle.
And we laugh. Then you are sick again.

This evening you sit in your usual chair
in the bloat of chemo, your breath really
bothering you. And me, if truth be told.
You are darning pullovers neither of us
ever wear – and even Oxfam won't take.

What if I could give you a new pair?
That will always pass the pencil test, even
at 90; with dark aureoles and pert
tips that tilt cheekily, but don't
show through your tennis dress.

You are muttering about camels
and licking the thread for the nth time;
specs half-way down – in your usual chair.
I don't see hacked-at womanhood,
that you've sobbed salt-herring barrels for.

I see you. Darning your way to normality.

TAMOXIFEN

ALISON MOSQUERA

My doctor's given me a massive can
of elephant repellent. I'm to spray

it, after washing, on my skin. It will
substantially reduce the risk, he says

of being trampled by an elephant
in Saville Row, The Side or Grainger Street.

I'm terrified of elephants, of course
but never have I seen one roam the streets

of Tyneside. That's the point, my doctor says
as if their absence proves the potency

of elephant repellent. Problem is,
the spray's a vivid blue and permanent

so I'd be branded like some miscreant –
my only crime, susceptibility

to elephant advances. Worst of all
I won't be able to forget my plight.

And how can I be sure the spray will work?
And how long must I use the wretched stuff?

Five years … that long? What choices do I have?
I spray, and hope, and bear the mark, or risk

the onslaught of an errant elephant
one unsuspecting day. Well, thank you, doc

but no, I won't be cowed: my life's too short
to waste in fear. Five years is far too long,

the benefit does not outweigh the risk.
Instead I'll stride out blithely every day

and if by chance I meet an elephant
perhaps I'll have some peanuts in my bag

and as it's said that they cannot resist
the taste of nuts, well, maybe I'll survive.

SMALL PLEASURES

ONE OF the themes that I came across again and again when I was putting together this book was the importance of savouring the moment. Wendy Cope sums this up in her poem 'Every', which summons up a sunny landscape and then casts the shadow of mortality in the last line. If there is a silver lining to pain and suffering, it must be that it teaches gratitude for the present, as Jo Shapcott writes in 'Procedure': 'say thank you thank you thank you for the then, and now'.

THE THRUSH'S NEST

JOHN CLARE

Within a thick and spreading hawthorn bush
That overhung a molehill large and round,
I heard from morn to morn a merry thrush
Sing hymns to sunrise, and I drank the sound
With joy; and often, an intruding guest,
I watched her secret toil from day to day –
How true she warped the moss to form a nest,
And modelled it within with wood and clay;
And by and by, like heath-bells gilt with dew,
There lay her shining eggs, as bright as flowers,
Ink-spotted over shells of greeny blue;
And there I witnessed, in the sunny hours,
A brood of nature's minstrels chirp and fly,
Glad as the sunshine and the laughing sky.

EVERY

WENDY COPE

Every ditch or stream or river the train crosses.
Every ploughed field, every row of trees.
Every square church tower in the distance.
Every minute of sunshine, every shadow.
Every wisp of cloud in the wide, blue, East Anglian sky.
Every day. Every day that's left.

OTHERWISE

JANE KENYON

I got out of bed
on two strong legs.
It might have been
otherwise. I ate
cereal, sweet
milk, ripe, flawless
peach. It might
have been otherwise.
I took the dog uphill
to the birchwood.
All morning I did
the work I love.

At noon I lay down
with my mate. It might
have been otherwise.
We ate dinner together

at a table with silver
candlesticks. It might
have been otherwise.
I slept in a bed
in a room with paintings
on the walls, and
planned another day
just like this day.
But one day, I know,
it will be otherwise.

Goes Without Saying

Bernard O'Donoghue

It is a great pity we don't know
When the dead are going to die.
So that, over a last companionable
Drink, we could tell them
How much we liked them.

Happy the man who, dying, can
Place his hand on his heart and say:
'At least I didn't neglect to tell
The thrush how beautifully she sings.'

CALLING THE KETTLE

DENNIS O'DRISCOLL

No matter what news breaks,
it's impossible to think
straight until the kettle has
been boiled.

The kettle with its metal back
strong enough to take the strain,
shoulders broad enough to cry on;

plump as the old grandmother
in her woollen layers of skirts
who is beyond surprise or shock,

who knows the value of allowing
tears to flow, of letting off steam,
of wetting the tea and, her hand

patting your cheek, insisting – as she
prevails on you to sit and drink – that
things could have been much worse.

CHEMOTHERAPY

JULIA DARLING

I did not imagine being bald
at forty-four. I didn't have a plan.
Perhaps a scar or two from growing old,
hot flushes. I'd sit fluttering a fan.

But I am bald, and hardly ever walk
by day, I'm the invalid of these rooms,
stirring soups, awake in the half dark,
not answering the phone when it rings.

I never thought that life could get this small,
that I would care so much about a cup,
the taste of tea, the texture of a shawl,
and whether or not I should get up.

I'm not unhappy. I have learnt to drift
and sip. The smallest things are gifts.

AFTER FROST

BRIAN PATTEN

It's hard to tell what bird it is
Singing in the misty wood,
Or the reason for its song
So late after evening's come.

When all else has dropped its name
Down into the scented dark
Its song grown cool and clear says
Nothing much to anyone.

But catches hold a whisper in my brain
That only now is understood.
It says, rest your life against his song,
It's rest enough for anyone.

JOURNEYWOMAN

ALISON MICHELL

I hadn't planned to go travelling
when – without warning – they sent me
on a journey to a land with no maps.
Sometimes I go on foot, climbing
slow stairs to the top of towers.
On other days I find myself blurring
through stations with unreadable names.

The lack of a guidebook disturbs me
at first. I want to know my destination,
time of arrival, will there be a bed?
But I've grown to like the unexpected:
a butterfly resting on a blue-painted door,
a walk on sand and seagrass.
Once I saw an eagle soar.

PROCEDURE

JO SHAPCOTT

This tea, this cup of tea, made of leaves,
made of the leaves of herbs and absolute

almond blossom, this tea, is the interpreter
of almond, liquid touchstone which lets us
scent its true taste at last and with a bump,

in my case, takes me back to the yellow time
of trouble with blood tests, and cellular
madness, and my presence required

on the slab for the surgery, and all that mess
I don't want to comb through here because
it seems, honestly, a trifle now that steam

and scent and strength and steep and infusion
say thank you thank you thank you for the then, and now.

VISITING HOURS

I**T'S A** by-product of medical advance that most of us have no idea of the etiquette of the sickroom. In the Victorian era chronic illness was a fact of life and people knew how to behave around it. Anyone who has ever been hospitalised will know how exhausting it is to have visitors who don't understand that you are not there to entertain *them*. Every ward should have a sign that says, 'If a patient wants to talk about their symptoms, they will.' The duty of the visitor is to make the time pass more brilliantly, or to be the bearer of such juicy gossip that even intimations of mortality are banished.

How to Behave with the Ill

JULIA DARLING

Approach us assertively, try not to
cringe or sidle, it makes us fearful.
Rather walk straight up and smile.
Do not touch us unless invited,
particularly don't squeeze upper arms,
or try to hold our hands. Keep your head erect.
Don't bend down, or lower your voice.
Speak evenly. Don't say
'How are you?' in an underlined voice.
Don't say, *I heard that you were very ill.*
This makes the poorly paranoid.
Be direct, say 'How's your cancer?'
Try not to say how well we look,
compared to when we met in Safeway's.
Please don't cry, or get emotional,
and say how dreadful it all is.
Also (and this is hard I know)

try not to ignore the ill, or to scurry
past, muttering about a bus, the bank.
Remember that this day might be your last
and that it is a miracle that any of us
stands up, breathes, behaves at all.

We drew lots, who would go and see him.
It was me. I got up from our table.
It was almost time for visiting hours.

He said nothing in reply to my greeting.
I tried to take his hand – he pulled it back
like a hungry dog who wouldn't give up a bone.

He seemed ashamed of dying.
I don't know what you say to someone like him.
As in a photomontage, our eyes would not meet.

He didn't ask me to stay or go.
He didn't ask about anyone at our table.
Not about you, Bolek. Not about you, Tolek. Not about
  you, Lolek.

My head began to ache. Who was dying for whom!
I praised medicine and the three violets in the glass.
I talked about the sun and thought dark thoughts.

How good there's a staircase to run down.
How good there's a gate to be opened.
How good you're all waiting for me at our table.

The smell of a hospital makes me sick.

THE UNPROFESSIONALS

U.A. FANTHORPE

When the worst thing happens,
That uproots the future,
That you must live for every hour of your future,

They come,
Unorganised, inarticulate, unprofessional;

They come sheepishly, sit with you, holding hands,
From tea to tea, from Anadin to Valium,
Sleeping on put-you-ups, answering the phone,
Coming in shifts, spontaneously,

Talking sometimes,
About wallflowers, and fishing, and why
Dealing with Kleenex and kettles,
Doing the washing up and the shopping,

Like civilians in a shelter, under bombardment,
Holding hands and sitting it out
Through the immortality of all the seconds,
Until the blunting of time.

FROM *A Wish*

MATTHEW ARNOLD

Spare me the whispering, crowded room,
The friends who come, and gape, and go;
The ceremonious air of gloom –
All which makes death a hideous show!

Nor bring, to see me cease to live,
Some doctor full of phrase and fame,
To shake his sapient head and give
The ill he cannot cure a name.

Nor fetch, to take the accustom'd toll
Of the poor sinner bound for death,
His brother doctor of the soul,
To canvass with official breath

The future and its viewless things –
That undiscover'd mystery
Which one who feels death's winnowing wings
Must needs read clearer, sure, than he!

Bring none of these! but let me be,
While all around in silence lies,
Moved to the window near, and see
Once more before my dying eyes

Bathed in the sacred dews of morn
The wide aerial landscape spread –
The world which was ere I was born,
The world which lasts when I am dead.

You Have to Laugh

W ELL, you don't have to laugh, but full-on grief is so exhausting. Everyone needs a little respite now and then. Cracking a joke as you go into the scanner may be a form of denial, but it feels a lot better than dumb misery. I love the image of the faithful angle-poised lamp 'waddling across the cemetery' in Billy Collins's poem 'Memento Mori'. There are lots of poems in this book that will inspire you (see the How to Carry On section), but the ones here are for when you just have to cackle in the face of the Grim Reaper.

My Funeral

Wendy Cope

I hope I can trust you, friends, not to use our
   relationship
As an excuse for an unsolicited ego-trip.
I have seen enough of them at funerals and they make me
   cross.
At this one, though deceased, I aim to be the boss.
If you are asked to talk about me for five minutes, please
   do not go on for eight.
There is a strict timetable at the crematorium and nobody
   wants to be late.
If invited to read a poem, just read the bloody poem. If
   requested
To sing a song, just sing it, as suggested,
And don't say anything. Though I will not be there,
Glancing pointedly at my watch and fixing the speaker
   with a malevolent stare,
Remember that this was how I always reacted

When I felt that anybody's speech, sermon or poetry
  reading was becoming too protracted.
Yes, I was impatient and intolerant, and not always polite
And if there aren't many people at my funeral, it will serve
  me right.

DELIVERY GUARANTEED

KINGSLEY AMIS

Death has got something to be said for it:
There's no need to get out of bed for it;
Wherever you may be,
They bring it to you, free.

THE VILLAGERS AND DEATH

ROBERT GRAVES

The Rector's pallid neighbour at The Firs,
Death, did not flurry the parishioners.
Yet from a weight of superstitious fears
Each tried to lengthen his own term of years.
He was congratulated who combined
Toughness of flesh and weakness of the mind
In consequential rosiness of face.
This dull and not ill-mannered populace
Pulled off their caps to Death, as they slouched by,
But rumoured him both atheist and spy.
All vowed to outlast him (though none ever did)
And hear the earth drum on his coffin-lid.
Their groans and whispers down the village street
Soon soured his nature, which was never sweet.

THE BLACK BOX

GAVIN EWART

As well as these poor poems
I am writing some wonderful ones.
They are all being filed separately,
nobody sees them.

When I die they will be buried
in a big black tin box.
In fifty years' time
they must be dug up,

for so my will provides.
This is to confound the critics
and teach everybody
a valuable lesson.

MEMENTO MORI

BILLY COLLINS

There is no need for me to keep a skull on my desk,
to stand with one foot up on the ruins of Rome
or wear a locket with the sliver of a saint's bone.

It is enough to realise that every common object
in this sunny little room will outlive me –
the carpet, radio, bookstand and rocker.

Not one of these things will attend my burial
not even this dented goosenecked lamp
with its steady benediction of light,

though I could put worse things in my mind
than the image of it waddling across the cemetery
like an old servant, dragging the trail of its cord,
the small circle of mourners parting to make room.

COFFEE IN HEAVEN

JOHN AGARD

You'll be greeted
by a nice cup of coffee
when you get to heaven
and strains of angelic harmony.

But wouldn't you be devastated
if they only serve decaffeinated
while from the percolators of hell

your soul was assaulted
by Satan's fresh espresso smell?

THE WATER EXTRACTOR

JULIA DARLING

I can't stop thinking about
that water extractor that Ann mentioned
as she was going out of the door,
that sucked the moisture out of rooms.

I have tried to imagine
its shape, its vast, thirsty tongue,
the sound of its vibrant recesses,
how it knows not to take everything.

Apparently many machines
are available for hire. Extraordinary.
What other machines are there?
Where is the catalogue?

I would like a spiritual cleanser,
an automatic comforter,
a sushi maker, a cat groomer,
a bath essence maker.

a polisher for my arterial corridors,
a machine for blasting rooms with mirth,
a portable bone strengthener,
and a fear shrinker, one for every room.

How to Carry On

THE POEMS here are the verbal equivalent of steroids – they restore vigour to the weariest frame. These are the words to read to yourself when you wake up in the small hours, nameless and not so nameless fears ricocheting round your head like pinballs. I am a great believer in the power of incantation; it's worth actually saying these poems out loud. Yes, you may feel self-conscious declaiming Christina Rossetti at 3 in the morning, but it really does help.

AT EIGHTY

EDWIN MORGAN

Push the boat out, campañeros,
Push the boat out, whatever the sea.
Who says we cannot guide ourselves
through the boiling reefs, black as they are,
the enemy of us all makes sure of it!
Mariners, keep good watch always
for that last passage of blue water
we have heard of and long to reach
(no matter if we cannot, no matter!)
in our eighty-year-old timbers
leaky and patched as they are but sweet,
well seasoned with the scent of woods
long perished, serviceable still
in unarrested pungency
of salt and blistering sunlight. Out,
push it all out into the unknown!
Unknown is best, it beckons best,
like distant ships in mist, or bells
clanging ruthless from stormy buoys.

CHE FECE ... IL GRAN RIFIUTO

C.P. CAVAFY

For some people the day comes
when they have to declare the great Yes
or the great No. It's clear at once who has the Yes
ready within him; and saying it,

he goes from honour to honour, strong in his
    conviction.
He who refuses does not repent. Asked again,
he'd still say no. Yet that no – the right no –
drags him down all his life.

WILD GEESE

MARY OLIVER

You do not have to be good.
You do not have to walk on your knees
for a hundred miles through the desert, repenting.
You only have to let the soft animal of your body
    love what it loves.
Tell me about despair, yours, and I will tell you mine.
Meanwhile the world goes on.
Meanwhile the sun and the clear pebbles of the rain
are moving across the landscapes,
over the prairies and the deep trees,
the mountains and the rivers.
Meanwhile the wild geese, high in the clean blue air,
are heading home again.
Whoever you are, no matter how lonely,
the world offers itself to your imagination,
calls to you like the wild geese, harsh and exciting –
over and over announcing your place
in the family of things.

GESTURE

CAROL ANN DUFFY

Did you know your hands could catch that dark hour,
like a ball, throw it away into long grass
and when you looked again at your palm, there
was your life-line, shining?

                    Or when death came,
with its vicious, biting bark, at a babe,
your whole body was brave;
or came with its boiling burns,
your arms reached out, love's gesture.

                          Did you know
when cancer draped its shroud on your back,
you'd make it a flag;
or ignorance smashed its stones through glass,
you'd see light in shards;
paralysed, you'd get up, walk;
traumatised, you'd still talk?

                          Did you know

at the edge of your ordinary, human days
the gold of legend blazed,
where you kneeled by a wounded man,
or healed a woman?
           Look –
your hand is a star.
Your blood is famous in your heart.

DAMAGED

DONALD ADAMSON

There's not a single tree in the wood
that isn't damaged.
Yet they grow tall and old
and when at last they fall they are noticed
not by their malformations
but by their absence, sudden blue
astonishments of sky.

Being is its own achieving.
The fabric of things
mends in spans accomplished and the joy
of particular wounds. Do not ask to be cured
nor pass your parcel of injuries
to others. You were damaged, let yourself
be changed, and grow, and live.

THE INSTINCT OF HOPE

JOHN CLARE

Is there another world for this frail dust
To warm with life and be itself again?
Something about me daily speaks there must,
And why should instinct nourish hopes in vain?
'Tis nature's prophesy that such will be,
And everything seems struggling to explain
The close sealed volume of its mystery.
Time wandering onward keeps its usual pace
As seeming anxious of eternity,
To meet that calm and find a resting place.
E'en the small violet feels a future power
And waits each year renewing blooms to bring,
And surely man is no inferior flower
To die unworthy of a second spring?

HYMN TO MASTECTOMY

CHRYS SALT

Here's to the woman with one tit
who strips down to her puckered scars
and fronts the mirror – doesn't give a shit
for the pert double breasted wonderbras
sneaking a furtive gander
at her missing bit.

'Poor lady,' they are thinking
'can her husband bear to touch her?
Will she ever dare to wear
that slinky low-cut sweater'?

Here's to the woman with half a bust
who wears her lack of symmetry
with grace and moist with lust
offers a single nipple like a berry
to her lover's tongue.

Here's to the single breasted ones
come home victorious from the wars,
wearing their wounds
as badges on the chests
of Amazons.

    'She ought to cover up
    it's embarrassing, it's shocking.
    I'm sure she thinks she's very brave
    but <u>everybody's</u> looking'!

Here's to those wondrous affrontages
out on the scene in sauna, pool and gym,
those who when whole were dying –
now less than whole
become themselves again.

HOW BRIGHT THE WIT

CHRISTOPHER REID

How bright the wit,
the circumstance-mocking
theatrical badinage, burned.
To a friend concerned
she might be tired
I heard her say,
'Exhausted people
leave the hospice all day,
and I just carry on talking.'

To another, catching
a glimpse of her own
undimmable spirit:
'I'm being radiant
again, aren't I!'

It was inspired,
brave, funny and subtle
of her to interpret
the role of patient
so flat against type –
cheering her nurses,
feeding advice and support
to friends, encouraging
her husband to address his
possible future
with something of her hope.

It's not in his nature,
but he can try.

 92

PHOENIX

D.H. LAWRENCE

Are you willing to be sponged out, erased, cancelled,
made nothing?
Are you willing to be made nothing?
dipped into oblivion?

If not, you will never really change.

The phoenix renews her youth
only when she is burnt, burnt alive, burnt down
to hot and flocculent ash.
Then the small stirring of a new small bulb in the nest
with strands of down like floating ash
shows that she is renewing her youth like the eagle,
immortal bird.

I Count the Moments

ELIZABETH JENNINGS

I count the moments of my mercies up,
I make a list of love and find it full.
I do all this before I fall asleep.

Others examine consciences. I tell
My beads of gracious moments shining still.
I count my good hours and they guide me well

Into a sleepless night. It's when I fill
Pages with what I think I am made for,
A life of writing poems. Then may they heal

The pain of silence for all those who stare
At stars as I do but are helpless to
Make the bright necklace. May I set ajar

The doors of closed minds. Words come and words go
And poetry is pain as well as passion.
But in the large flights of imagination

I see for one crammed second, order so
Explicit I need no more persuasion.

UPHILL

CHRISTINA ROSSETTI

Does the road wind uphill all the way?
Yes, to the very end.
Will the day's journey take the whole long day?
From morn to night, my friend.

But is there for the night a resting-place?
A roof for when the slow dark hours begin.
May not the darkness hide it from my face?
You cannot miss that inn.

Shall I meet other wayfarers at night?
Those who have gone before.
Then must I knock, or call when just in sight?
They will not keep you standing at that door.

Shall I find comfort, travel-sore and weak?
Of labour you shall find the sum.
Will there be beds for me and all who seek?
Yea, beds for all who come.

WHEN I HAVE FEARS THAT I MAY CEASE TO BE

JOHN KEATS

When I have fears that I may cease to be
Before my pen has glean'd my teeming brain,
Before high-piled books, in charact'ry,
Hold like rich garners the full-ripen'd grain;
When I behold, upon the night's starr'd face,
Huge cloudy symbols of a high romance,
And feel that I may never live to trace
Their shadows, with the magic hand of chance;
And when I feel, fair creature of an hour!
That I shall never look upon thee more,
Never have relish in the faery power
Of unreflecting love; – then on the shore
Of the wide world I stand alone, and think,
Till Love and Fame to nothingness do sink.

THE OLD STOIC

EMILY BRONTË

Riches I hold in light esteem;
And Love I laugh to scorn;
And lust of fame was but a dream
That vanished with the morn:

And if I pray, the only prayer
That moves my lips for me
Is, 'Leave the heart that now I bear,
And give me liberty!'

Yes, as my swift days near their goal,
'Tis all that I implore;
In life and death, a chainless soul,
With courage to endure.

Do Not Go Gentle Into That Good Night

DYLAN THOMAS

Do not go gentle into that good night,
Old age should burn and rave at close of day;
Rage, rage against the dying of the light.

Though wise men at their end know dark is right,
Because their words had forked no lightning they
Do not go gentle into that good night.

Good men, the last wave by, crying how bright
Their frail deeds might have danced in a green bay,
Rage, rage against the dying of the light.

Wild men who caught and sang the sun in flight,
And learn, too late, they grieved it on its way,
Do not go gentle into that good night.

Grave men, near death, who see with blinding sight
Blind eyes could blaze like meteors and be gay,
Rage, rage against the dying of the light.

And you, my father, there on the sad height,
Curse, bless, me now with your fierce tears, I pray.
Do not go gentle into that good night.
Rage, rage against the dying of the light.

Say Not the Struggle Naught Availeth

ARTHUR HUGH CLOUGH

Say not the struggle naught availeth,
The labour and the wounds are vain,
The enemy faints not, nor faileth,
And as things have been, things remain.

If hopes were dupes, fears may be liars;
It may be, in yon smoke concealed,
Your comrades chase e'en now the fliers,
And, but for you, possess the field.

For while the tired waves, vainly breaking,
Seem here no painful inch to gain,
Far back through creeks and inlets making
Comes, silent, flooding in, the main,

And not by eastern windows only,
When daylight comes, comes in the light,
In front the sun climbs slow, how slowly,
But westward, look, the land is bright.

The Peace of Wild Things

Wendell Berry

When despair for the world grows in me
and I wake in the night at the least sound
in fear of what my life and my children's lives may be,
I go and lie down where the wood drake
rests in his beauty on the water, and the great heron feeds.

I come into the peace of wild things
who do not tax their lives with forethought
of grief. I come into the presence of still water.
And I feel above me the day-blind stars
waiting with their light. For a time
I rest in the grace of the world, and am free.

To My Husband

WENDY COPE

If we were never going to die, I might
Not hug you quite as often or as tight,
Or say goodbye to you as carefully
If I were certain you'd come back to me.
Perhaps I wouldn't value every day,
Every act of kindness, every laugh
As much, if I knew you and I could stay
For ever as each other's other half.
We may not have too many years before
One disappears to the eternal yonder
And I can't hug or touch you any more.
Yes, of course that knowledge makes us fonder.
Would I want to change things, if I could,
And make us both immortal? Love, I would.

Lessons in Survival

PETER SCUPHAM

To stay good currency with your heart solvent,
Be a pink bus ticket used as a bookmark,
A maidenhair fern, pressed but eloquent.

Look for a hidey-hole, cosy or dark,
Where no peekaboo finger or eye can excite
A meddlesome bigwig to poke and remark.

Survival is mostly a matter of oversight.
Be an old pencil stub, a brass curtain ring.
Don't keep your lid screwed on too tight.

With luck, your neighbourhood fairy will string
You along as a glass bead, a silver key,
A saved blue feather from a jay's wing.

A person like you, a person like me,
Must contrive to find butter, but not too much jam;
Live happy and warm as a pick-a-back flea.

Don't be a new airport, the flag of Siam,
A battleship decked with bunting and trouble,
A three-volume novel, the Aswan High Dam,

To founder in foundries of smoke and pink rubble,
To swell and topple, absurd, indecent,
To puff and froth like an overblown bubble.

Be a bit too precious to throw away spent:
Be good for others or perhaps a lark.
Be a whispered name, not a granite monument.

THE WISDOM DIVIDEND

WHEN I was putting this book together I met someone who had been very ill but had come through it and was now in good shape. She said that although her illness had been ghastly, she wouldn't want to go back to being the person she had been before. 'I will always be grateful for the things I learnt when I was sick,' she said. I am not suggesting for a moment that anyone should be grateful for the malign stroke of fate that puts them in hospital or looking at an empty bed, but maybe, just maybe, there will be a flicker of reward.

My Prime of Youth is but a Frost of Cares

CHIDIOCK TICHBORNE

My prime of youth is but a frost of cares,
My feast of joy is but a dish of pain,
My crop of corn is but a field of tares,
And all my good is but vain hope of gain.
The day is gone and I yet I saw no sun,
And now I live, and now my life is done.

The spring is past, and yet it hath not sprung,
The fruit is dead, and yet the leaves are green,
My youth is gone, and yet I am but young,
I saw the world, and yet I was not seen,
My thread is cut, and yet it was not spun,
And now I live, and now my life is done.

I sought my death and found it in my womb,
I look't for life and saw it was a shade,
I trode the earth and knew it was my tomb,
And now I die, and now I am but made.
The glass is full, and now the glass is run,
And now I live, and now my life is done.

Calculations

WENDY COPE

I have been a non-smoker, now, for longer than I was a smoker.

I have been a published poet almost as long as I wasn't.

For more than half my adult years, I have earned a living without having a job.

I have been fatherless for nearly two-thirds of my life.

In the run-up to our wedding I reflect that I will not be a married woman for half as long as I was single.

But, if we are both alive when I am 96, I will have had as many years with you as without you.

Nearly a third of my life so far.

With luck, the fraction will grow, like sunlight spreading across a field from the west,

so the view at the end of the day
is brighter and more beautiful

than I could have foreseen
in the long, dark hours of the morning.

CANDLES

C.P. CAVAFY

Days to come stand in front of us
like a row of burning candles—
golden, warm, and vivid candles.

Days past fall behind us,
a gloomy line of burnt-out candles;
the nearest are still smoking,
cold, melted, and bent.

I don't want to look at them: their shape saddens me,
and it saddens me to remember their original light.
I look ahead at my burning candles.

I don't want to turn, don't want to see, terrified,
how quickly that dark line gets longer,
how quickly one more dead candle joins another.

WHEN DEATH COMES

MARY OLIVER

When death comes
like the hungry bear in autumn;
when death comes and takes all the bright coins from
   his purse

to buy me, and snaps the purse shut;
when death comes
like the measle-pox;

when death comes
like an iceberg between the shoulder blades,

I want to step through the door full of curiosity,
   wondering:
what is it going to be like, that cottage of darkness?

And therefore I look upon everything
as a brotherhood and a sisterhood,
and I look upon time as no more than an idea,
and I consider eternity as another possibility,

and I think of each life as a flower, as common
as a field daisy, and as singular,

and each name a comfortable music in the mouth,
tending, as all music does, toward silence,

and each body a lion of courage, and something
precious to the earth.

When it's over, I want to say: all my life
I was a bride married to amazement.
I was the bridegroom, taking the world into my arms.

When it's over, I don't want to wonder
if I have made of my life something particular, and real.
I don't want to find myself sighing and frightened,
or full of argument.

I don't want to end up simply having visited this world.

SWAN SONG

(FROM *THE GARDEN OF PROSERPINE*)

ALGERNON CHARLES SWINBURNE

We are not sure of sorrow;
And joy was never sure;
To-day will die to-morrow;
Time stoops to no man's lure;
And love grown faint and fretful,
With lips but half regretful
Sighs, and with eyes forgetful
Weeps that no loves endure.

From too much love of living,
From hope and fear set free,
We thank with brief thanksgiving
Whatever gods may be
That no man lives for ever,
That dead men rise up never;
That even the weariest river
Winds somewhere safe to sea.

FRANKLIN JONES

EDGAR LEE MASTERS

If I could have lived another year
I could have finished my flying machine,
And become rich and famous.
Hence it is fitting the workman
Who tried to chisel a dove for me
Made it look more like a chicken.
For what is it all but being hatched,
And running about the yard,
To the day of the block?
Save that a man has an angel's brain,
And sees the axe from the first!

LATE FRAGMENT

RAYMOND CARVER

And did you get what
you wanted from this life, even so?
I did.
And what did you want?
To call myself beloved, to feel myself
beloved on the earth.

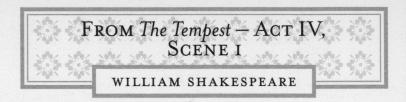

Be cheerful, sir:
Our revels now are ended. These our actors,
As I foretold you, were all spirits and
Are melted into air, into thin air:
And, like the baseless fabric of this vision,
The cloud-capp'd towers, the gorgeous palaces,
The solemn temples, the great globe itself,
Yea, all which it inherit, shall dissolve
And, like this insubstantial pageant faded,
Leave not a rack behind. We are such stuff
As dreams are made on, and our little life
Is rounded with a sleep.

PAX

D.H. LAWRENCE

All that matters is to be at one with the living God
to be a creature in the house of the God of Life.

Like a cat asleep on a chair at peace, in peace
and at one with the master of the house, with the mistress,
at home, at home in the house of the living,
sleeping on the hearth, and yawning before the fire.

Sleeping on the hearth of the living world
yawning at home before the fire of life
feeling the presence of the living God
like a great assurance
a deep calm in the heart
a presence
as of the master sitting at the board
in his own and greater being
in the house of life.

ON PRAYER

TRANSLATED BY ROBERT HASS

CZESŁAW MIŁOSZ

You ask me how to pray to someone who is not.
All I know is that prayer constructs a velvet bridge
And walking it we are aloft, as on a springboard,
Above landscapes the color of ripe gold
Transformed by a magic stopping of the sun.
That bridge leads to the shore of Reversal
Where everything is just the opposite and the word *is*
Unveils a meaning we hardly envisioned.
Notice: I say *we*; there, every one, separately,
Feels compassion for others entangled in the flesh
And knows that if there is no other shore
They will walk that aerial bridge all the same.

THIS

OSIP MANDELSTAM

This is what I most want
unpursued, alone
to reach beyond the light
that I am furthest from.

And for you to shine there –
no other happiness –
and learn, from starlight,
what its fire might suggest.

A star burns as a star,
light becomes light,
because our murmuring
strengthens us, and warms the night.

And I want to say to you
my little one, whispering,
I can only lift you towards the light
by means of this babbling.

JOURNEYS

R.S. THOMAS

The deception of platforms
where the arrivals and the departures
coincide. And the smiles
on the faces of those welcoming

and bidding farewell are
to conceal the knowledge
that destinations are the familiarities
from which the traveller must set out.

DAYS

PHILIP LARKIN

What are days for?
Days are where we live,
They come, they wake us
Time and time over.

They are to be happy in:
Where can we live but days?

Ah, solving that question
Brings the priest and the doctor
In their long coats
Running over the fields.

LEFT BEHIND

WHEN MY mother died, I took enormous solace from other people's memories of her. My sister read the wonderful Hardy poem 'Heredity' at her funeral and as I looked around the church at her siblings, children and grandchildren I felt the force of her 'in curve and voice and eye'. Mourning is not a linear process, the initial agony tails off, but you can find yourself derailed by slivers of recollection – every time I look at the Shard building in London I think of my mother pointing at it and laughing on the last car trip I made with her. Sometimes I can think of this without pain, and sometimes not. But I am glad that I have this reminder of her every time I look at the city's skyline.

Come Darkest Night, Becoming Sorrow Best

Lady Mary Wroth

Come darkest Night, becoming sorrow best,
Light leave thy light, fit for a lightsome soule:
Darknesse doth truly sute with me opprest,
Whom absence power doth from mirth controule.

The very trees with hanging heads condole
Sweet Summers parting, and of leaves distrest,
In dying colours make a grief-full role;
So much (alas) to sorrow are they prest.

Thus of dead leaves, her farewell carpets made,
Their fall, their branches, all their mournings prove,
With leavelesse naked bodies, whose hues vade
From hopefull greene to wither in their love.

If trees, and leaves for absence mourners be,
No marvell that I grieve, who like want see.

FROM *Ecclesiastes* CHAPTER 3
1568 BISHOP'S BIBLE TRANSLATION

BY MATTHEW PARKER

Euery thyng hath a tyme, yea all that is vnder the heaue hath his conuenient season.

There is a tyme to be borne, and a tyme to dye: there is a tyme to plant, and a tyme to plucke vp the thyng that is planted.

A tyme to slay, and a tyme to make whole: a tyme to breake downe, and a tyme to builde vp.

A tyme to weepe, and a tyme to laugh: a tyme to mourne, and a tyme to daunce.

A tyme to cast away stones, and a tyme to gather stones together: A tyme to imbrace, and a tyme to refrayne from imbracying.

A tyme to wynne, and a tyme to lose: A tyme to spare, and
a tyme to spende.

A tyme to cut in peeces, and a tyme to sowe together: A
tyme to kepe scilence, and a tyme to speake.

A tyme to loue, and a tyme to hate: A tyme of warre, and a
tyme of peace.

JULIA

WENDY COPE

1.
Julia, dear Julia,
taught me, one afternoon
in a shop in Chislehurst,
how to choose a card.
'That one is vulgar.
This one is too sweet.'

She's dead now
but her taste lives on.
I never buy a birthday or
a Christmas card
without asking myself
if she would approve.

2.
She rang me in the holidays
and told me she was doing

a chapter of Caesar every day.
I followed her example
and passed the exam.

The last time I saw her
she was dying, bravely,
of motor neurone disease.
She couldn't speak. She wrote notes
that made us laugh.

That's an example
I may need to follow one day –
harder than translating Caesar,
but, if I think of Julia,
perhaps I'll pass the test.

AFTER THE OPERATION

RORY WATERMAN

And there you were: awake, propped on the bed,
head up, knees up, smiling from a book,
the ward eerie with calm.
I don't remember what it was I said,
Mum, but I remember that you looked

eager, like I'd not quite seen before,
your big eyes shining as I came across
to touch your cheek to mine,
as love and hope cut free your albatross.
And this was what you had been fighting for.

WATER

CAROL ANN DUFFY

Your last word was *water*,
which I poured in a hospice plastic cup, held
to your lips – your small sip, half-smile, sigh –
then, in the chair beside you,

                         fell asleep.

Fell asleep for three lost hours,
only to waken, thirsty, hear then see
a magpie warn in a bush outside –
dawn so soon – and swallow from your still-full cup.

Water. The times I'd call as a child
for a drink, till you'd come, sit on the edge
of the bed in the dark, holding my hand,
just as we held hands now and you died.

A good last word.
> Nights since I've cried, but gone
to my own child's side with a drink, watched
her gulp it down then sleep. *Water.*
What a mother brings
> through darkness still
to her parched daughter.

AFTERWARDS

THOMAS HARDY

When the Present has latched its postern behind my
   tremulous stay,
And the May month flaps its glad green leaves like wings,
Delicate-filmed as new-spun silk, will the neighbours say,
'He was a man who used to notice such things'?

If it be in the dusk when, like an eyelid's soundless blink,
The dewfall-hawk comes crossing the shades to alight
Upon the wind-warped upland thorn, a gazer may think,
'To him this must have been a familiar sight.'

If I pass during some nocturnal blackness, mothy and
   warm,
When the hedgehog travels furtively over the lawn,
One may say, 'He strove that such innocent creatures
   should come to no harm,
But he could do little for them; and now he is gone.'

If, when hearing that I have been stilled at last, they stand
 at the door,
Watching the full-starred heavens that winter sees,
Will this thought rise on those who will meet my face no
 more,
'He was one who had an eye for such mysteries'?

And will any say when my bell of quittance is heard in the
 gloom,
And a crossing breeze cuts a pause in its outrollings,
Till they rise again, as they were a new bell's boom,
'He hears it not now, but used to notice such things'?

TAM CARI CAPITIS

LOUIS MACNEICE

That the world will never be quite – what a cliché – the
  same again
Is what we only learn by the event
When a friend dies out on us and is not there
To share the periphery of a remembered scent

Or leave his thumb-print on a shared ideal;
Yet it is not at floodlit moments we miss him most,
Not intervolution of wind-rinsed plumage of oatfield
Nor curragh dancing off a primeval coast

Nor the full strings of passion; it is in killing
Time where he could have livened it, such as the
  drop-by-drop
Of games like darts or chess, turning the faucet
On full at a threat to the queen or double top.

FROM *Long Distance*

TONY HARRISON

Though my mother was already two years dead
Dad kept her slippers warming by the gas,
put hot water bottles her side of the bed
and still went to renew her transport pass.

You couldn't just drop in. You had to phone.
He'd put you off an hour to give him time
to clear away her things and look alone
as though his still raw love were such a crime.

He couldn't risk my blight of disbelief
though sure that very soon he'd hear her key
scrape in the rusted lock and end his grief.
He *knew* she'd just popped out to get the tea.

I believe life ends with death, and that is all.
You haven't both gone shopping; just the same,
in my new black leather phone book there's your name
and the disconnected number I still call.

 134

REMEMBER

CHRISTINA ROSSETTI

Remember me when I am gone away.
Gone far away into the silent land;
When you can no more hold me by the hand,
Nor I half turn to go yet turning stay.
Remember me when no more day by day
You tell me of our future that you planned:
Only remember me; you understand
It will be late to counsel then or pray.
Yet if you should forget me for a while
And afterwards remember, do not grieve:
For if the darkness and corruption leave
A vestige of the thoughts that once I had,
Better by far you should forget and smile
Than that you should remember and be sad.

HEREDITY

THOMAS HARDY

I am the family face;
Flesh perishes, I live on,
Projecting trait and trace
Through time to times anon,
And leaping from place to place
Over oblivion.

The years-heired feature that can
In curve and voice and eye
Despise the human span
Of durance – that is I;
The eternal thing in man,
That heeds no call to die.

COMMON AND PARTICULAR

DAVID CONSTANTINE

I like these men and women who have to do with death,
Formal, gentle people whose job it is,
They mind their looks, they use words carefully.

I like that woman in the sunny room
One after the other receiving such as me
Every working day. She asks the things she must

And thanks me for the answers. Then I don't mind
Entering your particulars in little boxes,
I like the feeling she has seen it all before,

There is a form, there is a way. But also
That no one come to speak up for a shade
Is like the last, I see she knows that too.

I'm glad there is a form to put your details in,
Your dates, the cause. Glad as I am of men
Who'll make a trestle of their strong embrace

And in a slot between two other slots
Do what they have to every working day:
Carry another weight for someone else.

It is common. You are particular.

THE LAST HURRAH

THESE ARE poems of defiance, words that shake their fist at fate. Sometimes you just have to fight back, and these poems in their different ways are about blazing through life. I love the technicolour riot of Gerard Manley Hopkins's poem, 'Pied Beauty', and for Maya Angelou's anthem to resilience in the face of hardship, 'Still I Rise.' I think of these poems as a firework display – a splash of colour and passion piercing the darkness.

An Aspiring Spirit

AFTER QUEVEDO

DEREK MAHON

The final dark can take away my eyesight,
obliterating the white blaze of day;
it can release my soul and maybe gratify
the anxious hope of an eternal light —

but even on the farther shore it won't deter
the thought of where my earthly being burned:
blithely ignoring the strict rules, my fond
desire will swim back through the icy water.

The life that held such an aspiring spirit,
the arteries that fed so much impatience,
the marrow once so glisteningly bright

may wither, but their ardour will survive.
There will be ashes, yes, but smouldering ashes;
there will be dust, but dust glowing with love.

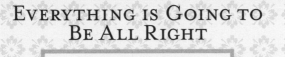

Everything is Going to Be All Right

Derek Mahon

How should I not be glad to contemplate
the clouds clearing beyond the dormer window
and a high tide reflected on the ceiling?
There will be dying, there will be dying,
but there is no need to go into that.
The lines flow from the hand unbidden
and the hidden source is the watchful heart.
The sun rises in spite of everything
and the far cities are beautiful and bright.
I lie here in a riot of sunlight
watching the day break and the clouds flying.
Everything is going to be all right.

STILL I RISE

MAYA ANGELOU

You may write me down in history
With your bitter, twisted lies,
You may trod me in the very dirt
But still, like dust, I'll rise.

Does my sassiness upset you?
Why are you beset with gloom?
'Cause I walk like I've got oil wells
Pumping in my living room.

Just like the moons and like suns
With the certainty of tides,
Just like hopes springing high,
Still I'll rise.

Did you want to see me broken?
Bowed head and lowered eyes?

Shoulders falling down like teardrops,
Weakened by my soulful cries?

Does my haughtiness offend you?
Don't you take it awful hard
'Cause I laugh like I've got gold mines
Diggin' in my own backyard.

You may shoot me with your words,
You may cut me with your eyes,
You may kill me with your hatefulness,
But still, like air, I'll rise.

Does my sexiness upset you?
Does it come as a surprise
That I dance like I've got diamonds
At the meeting of my thighs?

Out of the huts of history's shame
I rise
Up from a past that's rooted in pain
I rise
I'm a black ocean, leaping and wide,

Welling and swelling I bear in the tide.

Leaving behind nights of terror and fear
I rise
Into a daybreak that's wondrously clear
I rise
Bringing the gifts that my ancestors gave,
I am the dream and the hope of the slave.
I rise
I rise
I rise.

From *Holy Sonnets*

JOHN DONNE

Death, be not proud, though some have called thee
Mighty and dreadful, for thou art not so;
For those whom thou thinkst thou dost overthrow
Die not, poor Death, nor yet canst thou kill me.
From rest and sleep, which but thy pictures be,
Much pleasure – then, from thee much more must flow;
And soonest our best men with thee do go,
Rest of their bones and soul's delivery.
Thou'rt slave to fate, chance, kings, and desperate men,
And dost with poison, war, and sickness dwell;
And poppy or charms can make us sleep as well,
And better than thy stroke. Why swellst thou then?
One short sleep past, we wake eternally,
And death shall be no more. Death, thou shalt die.

PIED BEAUTY

GERARD MANLEY HOPKINS

Glory be to God for dappled things –
For skies of couple-colour as a brinded cow;
For rose-moles all in stipple upon trout that swim;
Fresh-firecoal chestnut-falls; finches' wings;
Landscape plotted and pieced – fold, fallow, and plough;
And all trades, their gear and tackle and trim.

All things counter, original, spare, strange;
Whatever is fickle, freckled (who knows how?)
With swift, slow; sweet, sour; adazzle, dim;
He fathers-forth whose beauty is past change:
Praise him.

INDEX OF EMOTIONS

147

148

150

INDEX OF FIRST LINES

INDEX OF POETS

CREDITS

Every effort has been made by the publishers to contact copyright holders of all the poems in this volume. The publisher will be glad to rectify any omissions at the earliest opportunity.

Page 2 'The Health Scare' by Wendy Cope reproduced by kind permission of the author; page 3 'End Game' by Brian Cox, published in *My Eightieth Year To Heaven* (Carcanet Press, 2007); page 4 'Gethsemane Day' published in *Gethsemane Day* by Dorothy Molloy (Faber, 2006); page 5 'Of Mutability' by Jo Shapcott published in *Of Mutability* (Faber, 2010); page 6 'Devonshire Street, W.1.' by John Betjeman from *Collected Poems* (John Murray, 2006); page 7 'What the Doctor Said' by Raymond Carver from *All of Us: The Collected Poems* (Harvill Press, 1997), reproduced by kind permission of Grove Atlantic and Atlantic Books; page 9 'Ultra Sound' by Penelope Shuttle from *A Leaf Out of His Book* (Carcanet Press, 2001); page 13 'Give me a Doctor' by W.H. Auden; page 15 'Waiting Room' by U.A. Fanthorpe, reproduced by kind permission of the estate of U.A. Fanthorpe; page 18 'Out-Patients' by Carole Satyamurti from *Stitching the Dark: New & Selected Poems* (Bloodaxe Books, 2005), reprinted with permission of Bloodaxe Books, on behalf of the author, www.bloodaxebooks.com; page 21 'Nurses' by Julia Darling, from *Apologies for Absence* (Arc Publications, 2004), reproduced by kind permission of Julia Darling's family; page 22 'How to Suss out the Night Staff' by Catherine Graham, reproduced by kind permission of the author; page 23 'Five O'Clock Shadow' by John Betjeman from *Collected Poems* (John Murray, 2006); page 24 'Nothing' by Selima Hill from *Gloria: Selected Poems* (Bloodaxe Books, 2008), reprinted with permission of Bloodaxe Books, on behalf of the author, www.bloodaxebooks.com; page 25 'Local' by Grey Gowrie from *Third Day: New and Selected Poems* (Carcanet Press, 2008); page 28 'After Visiting Hours' by U.A. Fanthorpe, reproduced by kind permission of the estate of U.A. Fanthorpe; page 30 'Ward Mouth' by Pat Borthwick, reproduced by kind permission of the author; page 33 'The Dog' by Hugo Williams from *I Knew the Bride* (Faber, 2014); page 36 'Brief reflection on the word Pain' by Miroslav Holub, from *Poems Before and After: Collected English* (Bloodaxe Books, 2006), reprinted with permission of Bloodaxe Books, on behalf of the author, www.bloodaxebooks.com; page 37 'Pain' by Elizabeth Jennings from *The Collected Poems* (Carcanet Press, 2012); page 38 'The Fish' from *The Complete Poems 1927–1979* by Elizabeth Bishop, copyright © 1979, 1983 by Alice Helen Methfessel, reprinted by permission of Farrar, Straus and Giroux, LLC; page 43 'Radiotherapy' from *Gethsemane Day* by Dorothy Molloy (Faber, 2006); page 44 'Prostate', by Brian Cox published in *My Eightieth Year To Heaven* (Carcanet Press, 2007); page 45 'Hairless' by Jo Shapcott published in *Of Mutability* (Faber, 2010); page 46 'Haiku' by Claire Knight; page 47 'Another box of nipples arrived today' by Char March, reproduced by kind permission of the author; page 49 'Tamoxifen' by Alison Mosquera; page 53 'Every' by Wendy Cope (Faber); page 54 'Otherwise' by Jane Kenyon' from *Collected*